Sendi Lee Mason

AND THE MILK CARTON KIDS

Other Crossway Books by Hilda Stahl

THE PRAIRIE FAMILY ADVENTURE SERIES
Sadie Rose and the Daring Escape
Sadie Rose and the Cottonwood Creek Orphan
Sadie Rose and the Outlaw Rustlers
Sadie Rose and the Double Secret

SUPER J*A*M ADVENTURES
*The Great Adventures of Super J*A*M*
The World's Greatest Hero

Sendi Lee Mason

AND THE
MILK CARTON KIDS

Hilda Stahl

CROSSWAY BOOKS • WESTCHESTER, ILLINOIS 60154
A DIVISION OF GOOD NEWS PUBLISHERS

Sendi Lee Mason and the Milk Carton Kids.

Published by Crossway Books, a division of
Good News Publishers, Westchester, Illinois 60154.

Cover design: John Seid

Cover illustration: Deborah Huffman

First printing, 1990

Printed in the United States of America

Library of Congress Catalog Card Number

ISBN 0-89107-547-X

*Dedicated with love to
Sonya and Lewis McNeely*

Contents

1

New Home

Sendi cringed against the side of the car as she saw Janice's jaw tighten. Sendi knew Janice was thinking about the huge fight she'd had with Momma last week, and she didn't dare argue when Janice got that look on her face. "I just said maybe we should go back and live with Momma."

Janice left the box teetering on the top of the others rammed in the trunk, whipped around, and shook her finger at Sendi. "Don't say that! Don't ever say that again to me,

Sendi Lee Mason! And don't you dare think you can go back on your own."

"I just said *maybe* we should go back." Sendi's voice came weakly.

"Well, we aren't going to. Not now and not ever!" Janice brushed an unsteady hand across her flushed, round face. "I'm twenty-two years old and it's high time I lived on my own."

"I'm nine. I can't live on my own."

"You're not on your own. You're with me. And where I go, you go! Understand?"

Sendi sighed. "I guess." But she didn't. She'd been happy enough living with Momma and going to school in Weston with kids she knew. Hardly any of them asked any more if she had a dad, and if she did, where was he. Now, she'd have to start fourth grade in a dumb new school with no friends and dumb people asking all kinds of dumb questions.

"Here. Take this." Janice thrust a box in Sendi's arms. "Don't drop it. It's your stuff you were so determined to bring."

Sendi clung to the box that held her old coloring books, crayons, birthday cards, school papers, a few photos of kids from third grade, some special rocks, and her birth certificate that she'd found tucked away in the kitchen drawer with Momma's recipe books. Neither Momma nor Janice knew she had it. At night if she couldn't sleep, she'd take it out and read it and hold it close and know that she really had been born. She wasn't adopted or from another planet or anything weird like some kids said. It was a real birth certificate just like the one Mrs. Tucker in second grade had shown them once.

Sendi stopped on the paper-dry, brown grass and stared at the tiny house that would be home from now on. Last year for Christmas she'd wanted a dollhouse bigger than this house tucked between two trees on the city lot. Of course she didn't get the dollhouse. Mom had said they were too poor for more than a new doll and a few school clothes. She closed her wide blue eyes, opened them, and looked at the house again. "I don't want to live here."

"You're going to."

"I know."

"I mean it, Sendi!"

Sendi waited until Janice stood beside her; then she looked right at her. "If you say so . . . Janice."

"Now, don't start, Sendi." Janice sighed as she set the box beside the door. "I won't let you make me feel guilty." She pushed back her blonde hair, tugged her blouse away from her plump body, and then rubbed her hands down her shorts. "Oh, it's hot. Even for August. Why didn't we move to a place that doesn't get this hot."

"You said this was the only place where you knew you'd have a job."

"I could work anywhere I wanted. Every town needs a good hair stylist. And I'm the best." Janice patted her neck and sent her dangling red and blue beaded earrings dancing.

Sendi turned away from Janice and away from the house. A white cat streaked under a bush in the yard next door. A brown-haired girl stuck her head around the side of the house, and Sendi stared at her with narrowed eyes. The girl jumped back out of sight. Sendi frowned. Music drifted from a house across the street, and then was blocked by a car driving past. Sendi kicked at the cracked sidewalk and muttered under her breath, "I hate it here."

"We got a lot of stuff to unpack, so we'd better hurry. It'll be dark soon."

"Do you have the key?"

"Of course. Mr. Prichard sent it to me in the mail. I showed it to you before we left Momma's." Janice's jaw tightened again. "I hope they turned on the electric. I told 'em to when I called yesterday."

Sendi looked around for the brown-haired girl, but she wasn't in sight.

Janice unlocked the door and pushed it open. Closed-in heat rushed out. She gasped and stepped back. "He said he'd open the windows for us, but he didn't." She wiped perspiration off her forehead and upper lip. "You might know you can't trust any man, not even a landlord that gets money from you every month for a house no bigger than a shoe box."

Sendi pushed the door wider and stepped into the living room. The smell sickened her as she looked at the worn plaid carpet, the ugly orange flowered sofa and chair, and then through the archway at the kitchen. She walked toward another open door to find a tiny bedroom with a small bed, mattress bare and stained, and a dresser with drawers hanging open. The room smelled worse than Momma's bedroom when she forgot to air it out.

Sendi set the box on the floor beside the

door and slipped her hands into the pockets of her stained shorts. She peeked inside another door to find a miniature bathroom and beside that another bedroom just a little larger than the first.

Janice walked past Sendi into the bedroom and dropped a box on the floor near the closet. Three hangers lay on wadded paper on the closet floor. "You take the other room, and I'll take this one since it has a bigger bed."

Sendi walked back to her new room and set her box on the foot of the bed. Dust puffed up and she coughed. She pushed open the lone window. A warm breeze stirred the limp curtains. Just then the same girl that she'd seen before peeked around a bush and once again ducked out of sight when she saw she'd been spotted. "What's her problem?" muttered Sendi, frowning.

"Sendi."

Sendi jumped and turned to see Janice standing in the doorway. "What?"

Janice locked her fingers together and cleared her throat. "You won't forget what we talked about on the way here, will you?"

Sendi's stomach tightened and slowly she shook her head.

Janice smiled stiffly. "Good. It's for the best. You'll see."

But she didn't see at all, not even after Janice had explained twice.

Janice turned and walked across the living room. "Come on and help me unload. I don't want to be doing this after dark."

Sendi bit her lower lip and rubbed her hand across her box. She knew the birth certificate was hidden safely away in the animal coloring book where she could find it quickly. How she'd like to touch it now and hold it against her heart!

Finally she walked to the door. She switched on the light and looked up to find it glowing softly overhead. "Good." She clicked it off, but not before she spotted the cobwebs hanging in the corners. She wrinkled her nose and ran outdoors just in time to see the girl that was spying on her jump out of sight. Sendi rammed her fists on her hips. "Hey, you, girl! Stop spying! You some kind of alien or something?"

The girl didn't answer, and Sendi ran to grab the box Janice held out to her.

2

On Her Own

Sendi drooped against the tiny kitchen table. "Can I go to bed now?"

"I told you all this cleaning has to be done tonight." Janice wiped her face with the corner of a green and white towel. "I have to go to work by nine in the morning, and I don't want to come home to a dirty house. Momma's not around to keep it clean like back . . . home."

For a minute Sendi thought Janice would cry, but she stiffened her back and turned to finish cleaning the last dirty drawer in the kitchen. Her shorts and blouse were streaked with dirt, and her hair that she usually kept neat and clean hung in dirty tangles around her plump shoulders. Sendi wanted to reach out and touch her to make her feel better, but she didn't move. "I don't know what else to do," Sendi said.

Janice turned with a frown. "Oh, all right then. Go take a shower and get to bed. Make sure you pull the shower curtain closed so water doesn't get on the floor. Be sure to use soap and shampoo. And get all the dirt off."

"I'm not a baby, you know."

"Well, you'll have to prove it tomorrow because you'll be spending the whole day alone."

Sendi stood very still and forced back the shiver.

"And I don't want you watching TV all day long."

"I won't." But she didn't say that she wouldn't have it on just for the noise. Being alone was scary. Back home she'd only been alone once in a while. Usually Momma had been there. Sendi glanced toward the refrigerator. "What will I eat?"

"I'll run and get a few groceries and bring

them back before I go to work. I'll be sure to get Wheaties and milk and stuff for sandwiches." Janice smiled and Sendi suddenly felt much better. "I might even get ice cream bars. You know, the kind you like."

Sendi smiled. "Thanks. And I won't eat the whole box in one day." She'd done that before and been spanked for it.

"See that you don't." Janice yawned and covered her mouth with her hand. "Go take your shower. I'll finish fast and we'll both be to bed before two."

Several minutes later Sendi slipped between clean sheets and watched the curtains blow out from the window. "I wonder if that girl is still outside spying on me. Or is she fast asleep in her own bed? I think I'll spy on her tomorrow."

Janice poked her head into the room. "Talking to yourself?"

Sendi giggled. "I guess."

"Tell yourself good night and go to sleep."

"Good night, self."

"Good night, Sendi."

"Good night . . . Janice." Sendi bit her lip. She'd almost said the wrong name, and she'd promised from this day on she'd always call her Janice.

"Sendi, I wish you didn't have to stay home alone. But I can't afford a baby-sitter, you know." Janice hesitated, and then walked away, leaving Sendi suddenly feeling more alone than she'd ever felt in her life.

Crickets blended together with a lone dog barking. The shower spray rose above the other sounds. Tears filled Sendi's eyes. She sniffed and blinked hard as she jumped out of bed, found her animal coloring book, and pulled out her birth certificate. She slipped back into bed and held the certificate to her heart.

The next morning she sat bolt upright and looked around. The sun shone through the window. Children shouted and laughed somewhere outdoors. Sendi jumped out of bed, and her birth certificate fell to the floor at her bare feet. She scooped it up and pushed it back into its hiding place. Then she slipped on blue shorts and a blue tee shirt with a rainbow on it.

Several minutes later after a bowl of Wheaties, Sendi ran out the back door into the small backyard. Weeds grew up around a sandbox made from an old tire. A row of bushes marked the line between her yard and the big backyard of the neighbors.

A sparrow flew from a bush onto a tree branch. The brown-haired girl peeked around the side of the house and Sendi jumped.

"Hey!" Sendi cried, pointing at the girl.

The girl ducked out of sight and Sendi raced after her.

"Hey, you! Come back here!" Sendi's thin legs pumped up and down and she swung her arms at her sides. "Don't run away!" But the girl had disappeared. Sendi stopped short in the front yard and looked all around. Her chest rose and fell. She doubled her fists. Sweat soaked her tee shirt and dampened her unbrushed blonde hair. Her blue eyes flashed with anger.

"She's being so dumb. So dumb," muttered Sendi. She walked slowly around the entire house and stopped again in the backyard. In the shade the grass was green. Everywhere else it was dry and brown. Raising her voice she said, "Dumb! You're playing a dumb spy game with me and I want you to stop it! Right now!"

Giggling, the girl stepped from behind a tree. "Hi. I'm nine and I live next door. My name's Gwen. What's yours?"

Sendi lifted her chin. "It's none of your

business. I don't talk to girls who play dumb spy games."

The girl shrugged and walked right up to Sendi. "I just wanted to get a good look at you. I might know you."

"How can you? We just moved in last night."

"I know. I watched you."

"I know. And I didn't like that at all!"

Gwen peered closer. "Blue eyes. Blonde hair. Eight or nine years old."

"Nine."

"And your name is?"

"Sendi."

"And you live with your mother."

Sendi frowned and swallowed hard. "With Janice. My . . . my sister."

"Oh?"

"So, what's wrong with that?"

Gwen shrugged a thin shoulder. "Nothing if it's the truth."

Sendi's face flamed. "What'd you mean by that?"

Gwen tugged her pink and white tee shirt over her pink shorts. "I have one purpose in life." She stopped and pulled out a notebook and a short pencil. "C*I*N*D*Y. Cindy."

"No. S*E*N*D*I."

Gwen frowned. "That's a silly way to spell Cindy."

"It's the name my mom gave me. And it's not silly!"

"But why did she spell it that way?"

Sendi thought for a minute and decided it wouldn't make trouble if she told Gwen. "My mom liked the name Cindy, and when I was born she had to spell it for the woman at the hospital. Mom couldn't spell very well and she thought since send was spelled s*e*n*d that Cindy must be spelled S*E*N*D*I. She told the woman to spell it that way. And I'm glad she did." Sendi had heard the story many times and enjoyed it more each time she heard it. "There's nobody in the whole world with my name."

"You're probably right about that." Gwen flipped through her book. "Are you sure that's been your name all of your life?"

"That's a dumb question." She peered at Gwen's notebook. "What're you looking at?"

Gwen held the notebook to her. "I told you I have one purpose in life. I am going to find missing children and get them back to their families."

"So?"

"So, how do I know you're not a missing child? I might've seen your face on milk cartons or TV or somewhere." Gwen squared her shoulders and looked right into Sendi's eyes. "I want to bring stolen children back to their families. If you're a stolen girl, I will return you to your family."

Sendi backed away. "You are weird."

Gwen shrugged. "I know. But I want to make a difference in this world, and that's how I'm going to do it."

Sendi had never heard anything so strange in all her life. "How are you going to find stolen kids?"

"I'll look for them. I memorize the kids on the milk cartons and other advertisements and I keep this notebook. I study every boy or girl I see unless I've known them all of my life. I check out everything about them until I learn if they're one of the missing children of this world."

"Well, you don't have to study me any longer. I mean it." Sendi's heart thudded hard against her rib cage. Somehow she had to keep Gwen from looking into her past. But how could she do it? Maybe Gwen would learn the truth, and all of Janice's great plans would be ruined. "You go find someone else to study."

"I will later." Gwen pushed the notebook into her pocket. "Want to play with me while you wait for your sister to get home?"

Sendi hesitated. "I might." She backed away. "Maybe I better not."

Gwen's dark eyes sparkled and she shook her finger at Sendi. "You're afraid I'll learn who you really are, aren't you? You thought I believed that wild story about your name. Well, I don't!" She stepped closer. "Now, who are you? Is your picture on a milk carton?"

Sendi ran into the house and slammed and locked the back door. She sagged against the wall, her hand clamped over her mouth.

3

Questions

"Sendi, what's wrong?" Gwen shouted through the door.

Sendi closed her eyes tight. "Go away!"

Gwen knocked. "You open this door and talk to me right now!"

"I can't!"

"Why?"

"I just can't!"

"Are you a milk carton kid, Sendi?"

"No." Giant tears welled up in her eyes and she blinked them away.

Gwen pounded on the door. "I think you are!"

Sendi jerked open the door and glared at Gwen on the step. "No! No, I am not! And don't you dare say that I am!" Her voice shook, and she knew any minute she'd burst into tears right in front of Gwen.

Gwen blinked and swallowed hard. Sendi saw the questions in Gwen's dark eyes. "I'm sorry, Sendi. I didn't mean to hurt you. I want to help you."

"Then don't ask any more questions."

Gwen reached out to Sendi, but Sendi backed away. "I do want to help you. Let me, will you?"

Sendi rubbed a knuckle across her nose. A car horn honked up the street. The smell of the cleaner Janice had used hung heavy in the air. "I don't need help."

Gwen studied her for a minute and finally shrugged. "Okay."

"I don't!"

Gwen moved from one foot to the other on the step. "Then you can help me."

"Oh?" Sendi leaned against the door frame with her arms crossed.

"You can search for missing children with me."

"Why?"

Gwen looked down at her dirty tennis shoes, and then into Sendi's eyes. "This kind of work gets lonely, you know."

Sendi pushed her tangled blonde hair away from her sweaty face. She motioned for Gwen to come in, closed the kitchen door, and leaned against it. "Then why do it?"

Gwen stopped in the middle of the room and turned back to Sendi, her dark eyes wide. "Because I have to!"

"Who's making you?"

Gwen walked to a kitchen chair and sat down. She looked up at Sendi until finally she sat down too. "All those kids that are missing are making me. They're scared and sad and lonely and away from the people who love them. Doesn't that make you want to cry?"

Sendi shrugged. "I never thought about it."

"Well, think about it." Gwen locked her hands together on the table near the sugar bowl. "What would you do if you were stolen away from your mom or your dad?"

Again Sendi shrugged. She'd never had a dad.

"You know you'd feel terrible! And so would I. So, I'm doing something about it."

"You're just a kid. What can you do?"

"I can try." Gwen jumped up and stood over Sendi with her hands on her thin hips. "So, do you want to help me, or not?"

Sendi tugged at the neck of her tee shirt. The silence of the house seemed magnified. "I guess it's better than staying here all alone all day."

"Are you going to be alone all day?" Gwen's voice rose in surprise.

"So what if I am? Janice is a hair stylist at Hair Care." Sendi poked out her chin.. "She didn't know anyone that could stay with me."

"Then come to my house and you won't have to be alone." Gwen brushed a strand of dark hair away from her sun-tanned cheek. "And neither will I."

"Where are your mom and dad?"

"Away for the day. They're high school English teachers, but in the summer they always have all these projects to do to keep active and keep on top of life. Mrs. Lewis is watching me." Gwen wrinkled her nose. "All she does is crochet and watch TV. She doesn't care what I do as long as I don't make noise."

"Are you the only child?"

Gwen nodded. "I always wanted brothers and sisters, but I never got them. How about you?"

"There's just me." Sendi picked at her thumbnail. Suddenly she jumped up. "Show me around the neighborhood and the way downtown."

"It's too far to walk downtown, but I'll show you around and take you to the corner store." Gwen stopped at the door. "Want to brush your hair first?"

Sendi touched her hair, and her face flamed. Without Momma around to remind her to brush her hair she forgot to do it. "I guess so. Be right back." She ran to her room, tugged her brush through her shoulder-length blonde hair, struggling with the snarls, tossed the brush back on the dresser, and ran to the kitchen. Gwen stood at the kitchen window, looking out where three boys were playing.

"Who are they?" asked Sendi.

"The Hansens. They live just in back of you in that big house with the big yard." Gwen turned away from the window. "I've known them all of my life. They're not lost or missing children. Come on. I'll introduce you."

"Oh, I don't know."

"Don't be afraid of them. They're okay. Shawn was my boyfriend for a while until he teased me about my great purpose in life." Gwen stepped outside. "My next boyfriend must be as interested in finding missing children as I am. Do you have a boyfriend?"

"No." Sendi scowled, remembering the time she'd liked Peter Gregory until he'd yelled at her for hanging around him. She'd never let herself like another boy. "I don't want to meet those boys."

"Oh, all right. They wouldn't stop wrestling just to meet a girl anyway."

Sendi watched them tumble together, laughing and shouting. How would it be to have a brother or sister to wrestle with?

"They aren't the only boys in the neighborhood." Gwen giggled and spun around, her arms wide and her brown hair flying out from her head. "I think I like Jason Richardson. He's so cute and he has blond hair and blue eyes and he talks to me a lot." Suddenly Gwen stopped and gripped Sendi's arm. "Look over there." She pointed to the house to the left of

Sendi's. "That's Diane Roscommon and she is not nice at all. She thinks she's beautiful and she plans on being a model. She has two younger sisters who are nice and two older brothers who tease me all the time. Diane is terrible!"

Sendi looked at Diane's long, brown neatly combed hair, clean red shorts, pink and red and white tee shirt, and red sandals. She looked nice to Sendi.

Just then a white cat walked into Diane's yard. She ran toward it, screaming, "You get out of my yard, you dumb cat!"

Gwen raced toward the cat. "Leave my cat alone, Diane. She's not hurting anyone!" Gwen scooped up the long-haired white cat and held it close in her arms. "Did she hurt you, Camille?" The cat purred and rested her head on Gwen's shoulder.

"Don't let that cat come in our yard again," snapped Diane. "I don't like cats." Diane glanced at Sendi. "Who's that? Who're you?"

"She's Sendi and she just moved in yesterday."

Sendi didn't like Gwen answering for her. She lifted her head and looked right at Diane. "I'm Sendi. I just moved in yesterday."

"Where'd you move from?"

Janice had said not to tell. "A long way from here."

Diane flipped back her long hair. "If you're going to be friends with Gwen, then you can't be friends with me. She's weird and I'm not, so you'd better choose me."

Sendi stepped closer to Gwen. "I won't choose you. So there! I choose Gwen because I'm weird too." Hadn't people told her that for as long as she could remember? This was the first time she'd met someone else called weird.

"Thanks, Sendi," said Gwen, smiling over her cat's head.

Blue eyes flashing, Diane walked right up to Sendi. "You chose wrong!" With one quick move she shoved against Sendi's chest with the palms of her hands and knocked her to the ground. "There!"

Stunned, Sendi cried, "Hey!"

"Stop that!" snapped Gwen.

"I'll do what I want." Diane tossed her head and looked smug.

"You'll be sorry!" Sendi jumped up, but Diane turned and fled into her house, slamming the door hard.

"Are you all right, Sendi?" asked Gwen.

34

Sendi nodded, her eyes glued to Diane's front door. "She is not nice."

"No. She's not."

Sendi brushed the dried grass off the back of her shorts. "Maybe she's a missing girl."

"She's not."

"If she was, I'd say let her stay missing."

Gwen giggled as she set Camille down on the ground. The cat rubbed against Gwen's ankle, then against Sendi's, and ambled off toward Diane's house. Gwen nudged Sendi's arm. "Are you ready to help me?"

"I'm ready." Sendi's blue eyes sparkled, and the corners of her wide mouth turned up into a smile. "Where do we start?"

4

The Search

Suddenly excited about the way her day was shaping up, Sendi ran along beside Gwen. Gwen's face was set with determination, and her doubled fists swung at her sides as she ran. "Where do we go first?"

"There's a family that just moved in on the next block. We've got to check them out."

Sendi hesitated. Just how would they "check out" a family? She caught Gwen's arm. "I won't spy. I mean it."

Abruptly Gwen stopped, blocking Sendi's way. "So, did I say you had to?"

Sendi shrugged. A car drove past. A path of sunlight streamed across the sidewalk and the dry grass beside it.

Gwen wiped a drop of sweat off her nose. "We'll walk right up to the door and talk to them."

Sendi rolled her eyes.

"They have two kids, a boy and girl about six or seven years old, maybe five and six."

"Did you watch them move in?"

Gwen nodded. "I watch everybody move in."

"That's spying."

"Spying for a good reason!" Gwen walked along the sidewalk, and Sendi fell into step beside her. "I tried to talk to them, but the woman that is pretending to be their mother said they had things to do and couldn't play with me." Gwen flung out an arm. "Play! Who wanted to play? Nobody understands."

"Why don't we forget the whole thing and go to your house and play a while. Do you have a video game?"

"No."

Sendi sighed heavily. "Neither do I."

Gwen caught at Sendi's arm. "There! There's the house and I don't see anyone in sight. Do you?"

"No." Sendi unlocked Gwen's hand and rubbed her arm. She studied the large white wood frame house. A porch wrapped around the front and one side. Huge trees shaded the yard and house, and a swing hung from one of the trees. Yellow and red and pink flowers bloomed in a circle of rocks. Someday she'd live in a house like that with lots of flowers, and she'd have a swing right in her own yard. Maybe she'd even have a dad to help pay the bills so Mom wouldn't have to work so hard.

"I'm going right up to the front door and ring the doorbell." Gwen sounded sure of herself, but she didn't move. She pulled her notebook and stubby red pencil from her pocket and held them close to her chest. "Yes, I am! I'm going right up to the front door and ring the bell."

Sendi cocked her head and studied Gwen. A dog barked in the distance and then was silent. A bird's song filled the air. "Are you scared?" That was a new and surprising idea to Sendi.

"No! Well, maybe a little."

"Then, let's get out of here." Sendi turned to go, but Gwen didn't move. Sendi turned back. "Well?"

"I just know something mysterious is going on in that house." Gwen nibbled the worn eraser on her pencil. "But I can't mess it up like I did last time."

"Last time?"

Gwen flushed. "We can't all be perfect, you know."

Sendi nodded. She'd said that many times, especially when her report card was bad or when she'd forgotten to carry out the trash for Momma. "What happened last time?"

Gwen was silent so long that Sendi didn't think she'd answer. Finally she said in a low, tight voice, "I was sure I'd found a missing boy, but I was wrong, and Mom and Dad got mad at me for calling the police to tell them. The policeman was mad too. So was the boy. And his parents."

Sendi started to tell Gwen how dumb she'd been, but the look of anguish on Gwen's face stopped her. "I sometimes make mistakes too," she said softly.

Gwen's eyes lit up as she smiled.

"Are you ready to go home now?" asked Sendi.

"No way! I'm going to talk to those people!" Gwen squared her shoulders, lifted her chin, and marched right up the sidewalk, up the steps onto the porch and right up to the heavy oak door. She pushed the doorbell and held her finger on it a little longer than necessary.

Sendi's stomach tightened. She took a deep breath and ran up to stand beside Gwen. Maybe nobody was home.

"If you think of any questions that I don't think of, ask them," whispered Gwen, her eyes glued to the door.

Sendi nodded and waited, her cold hands locked behind her back. She heard footsteps from inside and she wanted to turn and run, but for some reason she couldn't. She felt that Gwen needed her.

"Help me, Jesus," whispered Gwen.

Sendi shot her a surprised look just as the door opened, and a slender woman wearing jeans and a pink tee shirt stood there.

"Hello, girls. Oh, you again." She looked right at Gwen. "What can I do for you?"

Gwen held up her notebook. "I'm asking questions about all the kids in the neighborhood."

In the world was more like it, thought Sendi.

"And I'd like to ask your kids a few questions."

The woman smiled. "What kind of questions? They're pretty little to answer hard questions, but you could ask them what they like to eat or play or watch on TV."

Sendi looked from the woman to Gwen.

Gwen poised her pencil over her pad. "When were they born?"

The woman told her and she scribbled it down.

"Names?"

"Tommy and Star."

"Last name?"

"Langston."

"And your last name?"

"The same, of course." Mrs. Langston frowned slightly and moved from one sandaled foot to the other. From inside the house Sendi could hear kids shouting and laughing. Mrs. Langston glanced behind her and then back at Gwen. "I really am busy right now. I don't have time for your little game."

"Oh, it's not a game!" Gwen narrowed her eyes. "Are they adopted?"

"What a strange question. No. I gave birth to both of them." She slipped inside the door. "I really must go."

"Do you have their birth certificates?" asked Sendi all in one breath.

Mrs. Langston turned an impatient look on Sendi. "No. I do not. Now, I must get back to work!" She closed the door sharply, and Sendi turned to Gwen.

"Well?"

Gwen rubbed her notebook thoughtfully. "That was a good question, Sendi. I never thought of that before."

"I thought it was a good one." Slowly Sendi followed Gwen away from the house.

"I'm going to add it to my list." Gwen wrote as she walked. "It does seem strange that she doesn't have their birth certificates, doesn't it?"

"Very strange." Sendi thought of hers and wanted to hold it again, just to know that it was real.

"I am going to keep watching this house."

Sendi glanced back just in time to see Mrs. Langston walk out the door with two children. "Look!"

Gwen turned. "Strange. She said she had to work."

"Maybe she meant go to work."

"Let's follow them."

"How can we? They're getting in the car." Sendi stood quietly as the car drove down the street and turned a corner. She turned back to find Gwen watching her with a strange look on her face. Sendi bit her lower lip and waited.

Gwen stepped one step closer to Sendi. "Do you have a birth certificate?" Sendi's heart plunged to her feet. She crossed her fingers behind her back and tried to keep the color from rolling up her neck and over her ears and face. "No."

"You don't?" Gwen scribbled in her notebook.

"No!" She could never allow Gwen to see it.

"Very strange."

"Do you, Gwen?"

Gwen frowned thoughtfully. "I don't know. Let's go ask Mrs. Lewis if she knows."

Sendi breathed a sigh of relief as she raced after Gwen.

Suddenly Gwen stopped, and Sendi almost bumped into her.

"What?" asked Sendi.

"That house was empty yesterday and now someone's there," said Gwen.

Sendi looked at the small gray house with

44

black shutters. A boy stood at the large front window, a sad look on his face.

Gwen ran to the front door and knocked. Her eyes flashed with excitement. She flicked sweat off her forehead just as the door opened and the boy peered out. "Hi," said Gwen with a wide smile.

Sendi held her breath.

"Hi," said the boy. He had brown hair and huge blue eyes and wore overalls without a shirt.

"What's your name?" asked Gwen, her pencil ready.

"I don't talk to no stranger."

Sendi grinned. "Good for you, but we aren't strangers. We live just down the street. I'm Sendi and this is Gwen. What's your name?"

The boy thought for a long time. "Pete."

"Well, Pete, do you have a birth certificate?" asked Gwen.

Pete looked blank. "What?"

"How old are you?" asked Sendi.

He held up his hand with his fingers spread.

"Five," said Gwen, jotting in her book.

Just then a tall, lean man with a mustache loomed over Pete. "Hey, what's going on here?"

"She's talking to me," said Pete. "But they ain't strangers. They live on this block."

The man smiled, but Sendi saw the smile didn't reach his eyes. "Girls, if you're selling candy, we can't use any today."

"We aren't," said Gwen. "I'm Gwen McNeeley and this is Sendi. We want to get to know all the kids in the neighborhood. We'd like to get to know Pete."

"Maybe another day," said the man. He started to close the door, but Gwen held out her hand.

"What's your name?"

"Jack Thomason. Pete's dad." He pulled Pete inside and shut the door.

"Does he have a birth certificate?" shouted Gwen with her mouth against the door.

Sendi stepped back. "He's not going to answer. Let's go."

"We have three kids to check. I bet Pete is a missing boy. Doesn't he look like it to you?"

Sendi shrugged as she walked away from the house. "I don't know. I haven't studied milk cartons or other stuff."

"Well, you should."

Suddenly Diane jumped out from behind a tree and blocked the sidewalk. "Did you find another missing kid, Gwen?" she asked with a mean chuckle.

Gwen lifted her chin. "Maybe I did."

Sendi ran at Diane and shoved her backward, down onto the sidewalk. "You leave us alone!"

Gwen gasped and looked at Sendi in surprise.

Diane burst into tears as she scrambled to her feet. "You'll be sorry for that!"

"Oh, yeah?" Sendi doubled her fists, narrowed her eyes, and poked out her chin.

Diane backed away, and then turned and ran.

Sendi brushed off her hands and laughed. "There."

"I can't believe you did that!"

"I can't believe you didn't!"

Gwen shook her head. "My parents won't let me fight. We're Christians."

"Mom always told me to get in the first punch if I could." Sendi flipped her hair back. "So, I did."

"Where's your mom?" asked Gwen.

Sendi's heart jerked and she crossed her fingers behind her back. "She's dead."

5

Gwen's House

"She's dead." The words tore at Sendi's heart and throat and weakened her legs until she could barely stand.

"She's dead?" whispered Gwen, her hand at her mouth.

Sendi looked down the sidewalk at Gwen's house and just past it at her house. Heat waves shimmered above the ground. A sparrow dusted itself in a grass-free part of the lawn. Sendi's head spun. "I don't want to talk about it."

For once Gwen was silent until they reached her front steps. "We'll go talk to Mrs. Lewis and have lunch."

Sendi followed Gwen inside the one-story white house, cooled by an air conditioner, and then from room to room to see the house. The rooms were small, but clean, with nice furniture. The house looked more like a real house instead of the dollhouse she lived in now. It wasn't as big as Momma's though.

"And there's the window that I looked out when I first saw you drive up," said Gwen.

Sendi peered out Gwen's bedroom window at her house and her front yard. "It makes me feel funny to know you were watching me. I never thought about people watching me." What if she'd picked her nose or burst into tears?

"I watch everybody. It's my business." Gwen opened a dresser drawer and picked up a bundle of papers. "You can help me look." She dropped them on her blue carpeted floor and sat cross-legged in front of them. The wide bed, dresser, desk and book shelf that held toys and books took up so much room that there wasn't much floor space.

"What are they?" Sendi sank to her knees and looked at the thick pile of papers.

"Pictures of missing children." Gwen shuddered and blinked her dark eyes fast. "I can't stand it when I think about all the missing kids."

Sendi gingerly touched the top sheet. "I didn't know there could be so many kids."

"This is only part of them. Now it's up to us to see if the Langston kids are in here. Or Pete." Gwen suddenly sounded very businesslike as she picked up several sheets and handed them to Sendi. "Read the names and ages and look carefully at each picture. Some of them aren't very clear, and some of the kids have been missing only a few weeks, but others as long as eight years."

"Oh, my." Sendi looked at the top picture of a black boy named Justin. She knew he wasn't Pete or the Langstons, but she read about him anyway. He'd been gone for three years, and his own dad had taken him. Her stomach cramped. What if Mom had snatched her away from Dad? What if that's why Mom wouldn't talk about him at all, ever, no matter how much she asked?

Gwen glanced up from her search. "Did you find something?"

Sendi shook her head. "How do they know

Justin's own dad took him?" She tapped the page.

"Probably someone saw him. Some of the kids are taken from the parent that gets them after a divorce." Gwen's eyes narrowed. "Are your parents divorced?"

Sendi's ears buzzed, and a lump blocked her throat for a second. "Both . . . dead." But she didn't know if her dad was dead or alive or divorced or what. Sometimes the wanting to know rose up in her so big that she couldn't bear it. The first time she'd asked, Mom had said he was nobody worth knowing. But just last month she'd yelled, "I don't want to think about him or talk about him. Don't ever ask me again!"

Sendi ducked her head to hide her eyes and face, and Gwen didn't ask another question. Sendi pushed Justin's sheet aside and read the next one and the next.

"This might be the Langston kids." Gwen held out a sheet with a photo of a boy and girl together. "Don't you think they look like Tommy and Star?"

Sendi leaned close and studied the picture. "It' s hard to say. Those kids are three and four."

"But look at his mouth." She tapped the boy's mouth. "See that little dimple right at the corner of his mouth? It looks like Tommy to me."

"But the girl looks different. She has black hair."

"It's hard to judge in a black and white. I'll set it aside and keep looking." Gwen rubbed a hand over her knee and reached for another sheet.

Just then Mrs. Lewis stuck her gray head in the door. Sendi had met her when they'd first walked in. "Girls, lunch is ready in the kitchen. Fruit plate and chicken sandwiches."

Gwen jumped up. "Did you look for my birth certificate?"

Mrs. Lewis rubbed her hands over her wrinkled arms. "I told you I couldn't be going through your folks' private papers."

"Tell me where to look and I'll look."

Mrs. Lewis tapped the tip of Gwen's nose. "You'll have to wait and talk to your parents."

Gwen sighed and shrugged. "I guess I'll have to wait. Let's go eat, Sendi."

Her stomach growled with hunger as she followed Gwen to the kitchen. At her house Sendi knew she would've had a bologna sandwich and an ice cream bar. She wanted to ask what a fruit plate was, but she waited until she saw it sitting on the table. She looked it over, embarrassed that she didn't even know what some of it was. Mrs. Lewis had set a tiny bouquet of blue and white flowers in the center of the table. Two places were set with two clear-glass plates at each one, one filled with cut-up fruit on a lettuce leaf and the other with toasted wheat bread with chicken, lettuce, and a slice of tomato. Glasses of milk were set beside the sandwich plate. Yellow napkins were folded under the forks.

Sendi sat down slowly, her eyes on the food. Even Momma had never fixed anything that looked this good.

"I'll pray," said Gwen.

Sendi never prayed before she ate, but she bowed her head.

"Heavenly Father, thank You for my new friend, Sendi. Thank You for the beautiful day. Keep the missing children safe and help them to get back home again. And thank You for this food. In Jesus' name, amen." Gwen smiled across the small kitchen table at Sendi. "I always pray for the missing kids. Will you do it too from now on?"

Sendi nodded as she picked up her fork to stab into a chunk of watermelon, a piece of fruit that she recognized. She'd only prayed at bedtime when Momma had reminded her.

Gwen swallowed a bite of sandwich. "I know where Mom and Dad keep their important papers, and I'll look at them after we eat, when Mrs. Lewis is taking a nap." Gwen leaned forward and whispered, "She always takes a short nap after lunch."

Puzzled, Sendi looked around. "Why didn't she eat with us?"

"She likes her privacy when she eats. Her teeth don't fit right and they move when she chews. She hates it when people see her teeth flop up and down in her mouth." Gwen ate a strawberry. "I just decided what I'll do."

"What?"

"I'll find my own birth certificate."

Later Sendi followed Gwen into a bedroom that she said her parents had turned into a study. It held two desks, two chairs, a couch, a filing cabinet, a map of the world on the wall between two windows, and a typewriter on one desk. Flowering plants and green bushy plants stood on a wooden plant stand in a corner near the closet.

Gwen opened a drawer on the white metal desk and looked through several file folders. "I know this is the special drawer. I've been in here while they talk about insurance and credit cards and bills that need to be paid and stuff like that." She finally lifted one out. "It's marked CERTIFICATES," she whispered, her eyes wide and her hand trembling. "I don't know why I didn't think of this sooner."

"Why?"

"I have always thought I belonged to other people." She looked through the folder and read off what she found. "This is strange. It's a certificate stating that Tess and Henry McNeeley qualified as adoptive parents." The color drained from Gwen's face. "Adoptive parents!"

"Did they adopt a kid?"

"Me! Probably me! I'm the only child in this house!" Gwen leaned back in the chair, and tears welled up in her eyes. "I can't believe they adopted me and didn't even tell me!"

"You don't know for sure."

"Just who are my real parents?"

Sendi bit her bottom lip. She knew how Gwen felt.

"This is the worst day of my life." Gwen

knuckled away her tears. "What am I going to do?"

"See if you do have a birth certificate."

Gwen fumbled with the file and finally found her birth certificate. Sendi leaned close to read it. Gwen shuddered. "It says my parents are Tess and Henry. But are they really? I've heard that people that steal kids have fake birth certificates made for them." She dropped the certificate to the desk and stared wide-eyed at Sendi. "Maybe this is fake and I'm stolen from someone!"

"Or maybe you're only adopted and they didn't tell you."

Gwen took a deep breath and blinked hard and fast. "Why wouldn't they tell me?"

"Lots of reasons." But Sendi couldn't think of one.

"Maybe they changed their minds and decided they really didn't want me but couldn't take me back like you can a pet from the animal shelter."

Sendi moved restlessly, frantically hunting in her head for words of comfort, but found none.

Gwen glanced around the room, a pinched look around her mouth. "Sometimes I've watched them together, and they are so together that it feels like there's no place for me. They teach school together, ride home together, check over test papers together, eat together, sleep together, and go on missions of mercy for others together. And I get left with Mrs. Lewis." Tears slipped from Gwen's dark eyes and slid down her sun-tanned cheeks. "I think the only thing I can do is look for myself in all of my files of missing children. I might find me."

"Oh, Gwen."

"I might find me and return myself. Who would laugh at me then for my great mission in life?"

Sendi moved from one foot to the other. "I think I 'd better go home."

"Me too. If I could find my home."

"You might be wrong about all of this." Sendi tapped the birth certificate. "Ask your parents."

"Tess and Henry McNeeley, you mean."

Sendi nodded. "I'm going now."

Gwen slipped the certificate back into the folder and dropped the file in place in the drawer. "I'll see you later. I'll tell you if I find myself in my pile of missing children." Her mouth turned down at the corners, and all the color drained from her face.

Sendi laced her fingers together and looked helplessly at Gwen. Finally she ran from the room, down the hall to the front door and out. The heat struck her, and soon sweat soaked her clothes. She slipped inside her back door to closed-in heat that made her long for Momma's cool house.

Sendi cupped her hands around her mouth and tilted her head back. "Sendi Lee Mason is here. Is anybody else?"

6

A Talk with Janice

Sendi turned from watching TV to see Janice sagging in the doorway. For two days she'd watched TV and stayed away from Gwen.

"I'm beat." Janice pulled off her uniform and flung it over the back of the couch. Then she sat down with her slip pulled up over her round knees. "That's better." She dabbed her face with a tissue. "What did you do all day, Sendi? You didn't sit here in front of that TV, did you?"

Sendi clicked it off and sat on the floor with her back against it. "No. I was outside a while."

"I thought about you and wondered about you. I wish things could be different."

So did Sendi. "I was okay," she said. But was she ever okay?

"Well, I wasn't. You wouldn't believe some of those customers. I trimmed a man's beard today, and he complained to my boss that I cut it too short! He said he wanted it to look neat and tidy. So I cut it neat and tidy. He said I practically scalped him! Men! You can't ever please them."

Sendi glanced toward the window and thought of Gwen. Several times she'd wanted to talk to Gwen to see what she'd learned, but she was afraid of what she'd hear. She glanced over and watched Janice fan herself with a section of the newspaper. "Do you ever think about missing kids?"

"Me? Naw. Well, maybe sometimes when I see it on the news or see a poster. Most of the time I got too many worries of my own to think about other people's troubles."

"I think about missing kids."

"Oh?"

"I think about how awful it would be to be kidnapped by some stranger." Sendi looked down at her sandals and then over at Janice. "Or by your own dad or mom."

Janice patted her neck and sent her earrings dancing. "I wonder what I should fix for supper."

Sendi locked her hands around her knees. "Do you know anyone who's been kidnapped?"

"What? Oh, I never thought about it. I don't think so."

"I might know someone."

Janice leaned forward with a scowl. "Sendi, I think you're imagining things. What ever got you to think about this?"

"Just things."

"I think I'll make scrambled eggs or maybe a macaroni salad."

Sendi tightened her whole body and forced out, "Did you kidnap me from my dad?"

Janice sat bolt upright. "What?"

"Did you kidnap me from my dad?"

"That's a dumb thing to say! A terrible thing to say!" Janice stabbed her fingers through her hair and messed up her carefully styled strands.

Sendi hugged her bare legs so tight

against her chest she could feel her heart pump against them. "Did you?" she whispered around the terrible lump in her throat.

Janice jumped up, her eyes blazing. She flung her arm out and pointed toward the front door. "Go outside and play and leave me alone. When you're ready to eat and not talk about your dad, you can come back in."

Sendi wanted to stand her ground and shout right back, but she turned and stumbled out the door, a bright red circle on each cheek. The door slammed behind her and the sun blazed before her. She crept to the shade and leaned weakly against a tree. "I will find out about my dad," she whispered through gritted teeth.

She heard a sound and she looked up to find Pete standing a few feet away, watching her, his face flushed and tears on his lashes. "What d' you want?" she snapped.

He trembled. "Are you a stranger?" he asked in a voice so low she could barely hear.

She scowled and walked toward him, but he backed away. "You know me, Pete. I was at your house the other day. I'm Sendi."

Pete knuckled tears from his eyes and looked at her again with wide questioning eyes. Finally he nodded and relaxed a little. "You're no stranger. You live near me. I can talk to you."

"Yes, you can."

"I tried to catch a kitty and it ran away from me. I wanted to pet the kitty." He looked around helplessly. "I got to go home and I don't know how to find it."

Sendi saw the tears well up in his eyes, and she suddenly wanted to hold him close and cry right along with him. She bent down to him. "I can get you home. I know where you live." She took his hand and rubbed the back of it. His skin was as soft as a cotton ball and almost as white.

"Will you hurt me?" asked Pete.

"Hurt you? No! I'll help you," said Sendi.

Pete twisted the tail of his tee shirt around a small finger. "Daddy said strangers might hurt me."

"But I'm not a stranger."

"I forgot." He pulled his hand free and rubbed his face, leaving a streak of dirt.

She caught his hand and turned it over. A round red mark about the size of her thumbnail stained the inside of his wrist. "Did you hurt yourself?"

He peered down at his wrist and finally shook his head. "Daddy says that's always been there. He said he saw it when he first saw me in the hospital."

Sendi rubbed it, but it didn't rub off. "That's funny."

He pulled free. "No, it's not."

"I guess you're right. Come on. I'll take you home."

"Daddy'll be mad that I ran after a cat and got lost."

"He'll be glad to see you." She looked closely at him. "Won't he?"

Pete nodded. "Glad and mad both."

Sendi walked to the sidewalk. He followed and slipped his hand into hers. A tingle ran over her body. She held his tiny hand firmly and suddenly felt very grown-up and important.

She glanced at Gwen's house as they walked past. A car stood in the driveway, but no one was in sight. Maybe Gwen was talking to her parents right now to see if they really were her parents.

Pete squeezed Sendi's hand. "I like you."

"You do?" Sendi smiled, suddenly feeling happy for the first time in a long time. "I like you, too."

"Someday maybe you can come play with me."

"Your daddy might not let me."

Pete stopped. "I'll stick out my lip like this and act like I'm going to cry, and then he'll let you."

Sendi laughed. "Does that always work?"

"I did it so I could play outside when he was too busy to come with me. He let me play out and he said I had to stay in the backyard. I tried to stay, but I saw the kitty and I wanted to touch it, and it ran away from me. Do you know where it went?"

"Was it white?" asked Sendi.

"Yes."

"It belongs to Gwen. She lives right back there, and she was with me at your house the other day."

"Gwen," Pete said.

"Yes."

"She's not a stranger."

"No," said Sendi.

"I'll ask her if I can touch her kitty and she'll say yes, I bet." Pete smiled.

"I'm sure she will. Here's your house." She stopped on the sidewalk and turned to face the way they'd come. Heat shimmered off the sidewalk. Piano music drifted out from a house across the street. "See back there? That house belongs to people I don't know, and the next house is Gwen's and the next one mine. Now you won't get lost again if you walk down there."

Pete studied the houses. Finally he looked up at Sendi. "One day will you come play with me? I got cars and a sandbox."

She nodded. "I'll come if your daddy will let me."

"He will."

She squeezed his hand and then let it go. "See you later, Pete."

He flung his arms around her and hugged her.

She hugged him back and blinked hard to keep tears from falling. The last time she'd been hugged was when Momma hugged her because they were going away. In her house they didn't get hugged and kissed like in TV families.

Finally Pete pulled away. "Bye." He ran around the house, and Sendi slowly turned and walked down the sidewalk.

A boy whizzed by on his bicycle. With a sharp pang of regret Sendi thought about the old bike that she'd left at Momma's because it wouldn't fit in the car. Janice had said that as soon as she could, she'd buy her another one.

"That old thing's ready to fall apart anyway," Janice had said.

Sendi had rubbed the rusty handlebars. She knew that she'd never have a bike that she loved like that one. She'd learned to ride on it, first with training wheels and then without. Momma had bought it at a yard sale for five dollars. "I want my bike back," she whispered.

She stopped in the shade of a tall tree in Gwen's yard and looked at the house. The car was gone from the driveway. A water sprinkler flipped water over the lawn, keeping it green. From time to time, Sendi could see a rainbow of bright colors.

"You looking for Gwen?"

Sendi whipped around to see Diane standing there. Sendi stiffened, waiting for an attack that didn't come. Finally she nodded.

"She went somewhere with her parents."

Sendi rubbed her hands down her shorts. "How come you're not mad at me?"

"I am."

"You don't sound like it."

Diane shrugged. Dirt streaked her sun-tanned face and arms. Her yellow flowered sunsuit had a tiny rip in the leg. "How come you pushed me down the other day?"

"Because you pushed me down first."

"I won't do it again if you won't."

Sendi shrugged. "Okay."

"Want to play?"

"I have to go home to eat supper." Janice was probably over being mad and would have supper waiting.

"Your mom's fat."

Sendi's stomach tightened. "My mom?"

"Isn't the lady you live with your mom?"

"My sister," said Sendi.

"Oh. She's fat."

"I know."

"My sisters aren't. Neither is my mom." Diane looked proud.

"So?"

"Neither is Gwen's mom."

"Who cares?" Sendi scowled.

"Where's your mom?" asked Diane.

Sendi crossed her fingers behind her back. "She's dead."

"She get killed in a car wreck? I know a lady that did."

Sendi moved restlessly. "I don't want to talk about it. I'm going home."

"Come out and play after you eat. We'll play in my tree house."

Sendi looked suspiciously at Diane. "How come you're being nice?"

"I want somebody to play with."

"Why me?"

"There's nobody else to ask," said Diane.

The thought of playing in a tree house sounded like fun, and finally Sendi nodded. "I'll play with you. But you have to be nice to me."

"I will be. If you're nice to me."

"I will be. See you later." Sendi ran around the house to the back door. She took a deep breath and walked in. Janice turned from the refrigerator with a smile.

"I'm back," said Sendi.

"Good."

Relief slid over Sendi and she smiled too.

"Supper's ready. Set the table, will you?"

Sendi ran to the sink to wash her hands. Over her shoulder she said, "I made a new friend. Three new friends."

"Good. So did I. This one girl that works with me. Her name's Pepper. Isn't that funny?

Who'd name a girl Pepper? Anyway, she's almost as good as me with giving perms." Janice set the macaroni and cheese on the table beside the sliced cucumbers and tomatoes. "That Pepper. She's some character. She thinks I am some kind of saint for taking care of my little sister."

Sendi gripped the plates tighter as she carried them to the table.

"It made me feel good."

Sendi carefully set the plates and forks in place and turned to fill the glasses with water.

7

Discovery

Slowly Sendi walked across her yard toward Diane's. Once again the Hansen boys were wrestling in their backyard. They stopped and ran to Sendi. She wanted to sink out of sight, but she faced them, her heart racing and her knees knocking.

"Hi. We know you're Sendi," said the biggest boy. They all looked alike, thin with dark hair and eyes. "I'm Shawn. That's Teddy and the little one is Bruce."

"I'm seven," said Bruce.

"Want to play soccer?" asked Teddy.

"Not right now." She felt strange having the boys talk to her as if they were old friends. "I'm going to play with Diane in her tree house."

"You are? That's a giant surprise. We'll go with you," said Shawn, walking along beside Sendi. "It's Diane's turn to play in the tree house, and I'll see if she'll let us play."

"She never does," said Teddy, falling into step between Sendi and Shawn.

"She might today," said Bruce.

Sendi stopped at the bottom of the tree and looked up at the large wooden tree house. "Diane, I'm here."

Diane peeked out, and then scowled. The maple leaves shielded her from the sun. "What're you boys doing here? You can't play when it's my turn up here and you know it. You take turns when Allen and Donny do."

"How come you're letting Sendi play with you?" asked Shawn.

"I feel like it, that's why." Crooking her finger, Diane beckoned to Sendi. "Come on up."

Sendi looked up, up at the boards nailed over a thick branch. Was it really safe?

"You're not scared to climb the ladder, are

you?" asked Diane as if she couldn't believe her eyes.

"No." But Sendi didn't know if she was or not.

"We'll catch you if you fall," said Bruce, standing at the base of the tree beside the boards nailed to the tree.

"She's not going to fall," snapped Diane.

"I'm not going to fall," said Sendi. She carefully climbed up, the boards rough against her palms, and stepped out on the floor of the tree house. Her head spun and she stepped away from the edge. She felt as if she were on a green skyscraper.

Diane nudged Sendi's shoulder. "Are you going to faint?"

"No. I'm just a little dizzy. I've never been in a tree house before."

"Never? Where're you from? The moon or what?"

Sendi ducked her head. How many times had kids asked if she was from outer space because she couldn't join clubs or stay after school and play, and often she didn't know about the music or games they talked about.

Diane picked up a pad of paper. "Do you want to play school?"

"I guess."

"I'll be the teacher and you'll be the student." Diane shook her finger at Sendi. "And you better not be sassy or you'll have to stand in a corner."

Sendi carefully sat on the wooden floor and took the paper and pencil Diane handed her.

"We'll play school with you girls," shouted Shawn. "Won't that be fun, Diane?"

She peeked over the edge. "No! Now, go home before I tell on you."

"Why can't they come up?" asked Sendi.

Diane whipped around. "This is my tree house and I make the rules! I don't want those boys up here."

Sendi looked toward the ladder. She should've stayed far away from Diane. Maybe she should climb down and leave Diane alone.

Once again Diane peered over the edge. "Go home right now, you Hansen boys. I mean it!"

Sendi heard their angry words as they ran out of the yard. "I think I'll go too," Sendi said.

"No way!" Diane pushed her back down. "We're playing school. So, write your name at the top of the paper. And write it so I can read it."

"You said you'd be nice to me."

"I am being nice. Now, write your name!"

Sendi gripped the pencil tighter, but wouldn't write her name. Somehow she had to get away from Diane before Diane got mad and pushed her out of the tree house.

"Sendi! I've been looking all over for you. Come here quick!"

Sendi jumped up. "It's Gwen!"

"Get away from here, Gwen!" shouted Diane angrily.

Sendi looked over the side to find Gwen waving a paper.

"Great news! Come on, Sendi! Hurry," called Gwen.

"She can't play with you!" cried Diane, grabbing Sendi's arm.

"I'm not playing. This is work!" Gwen started up the ladder, but Diane yelled for her to stop.

"I didn't invite you up, Gwen McNeeley, so go back down right now!"

Sendi watched as Gwen hesitated, and then dropped to the ground.

"I need you, Sendi," said Gwen, dancing from one foot to the other.

"I'll be right down, Gwen." Sendi pushed

Diane aside and scrambled down with Diane right behind her, stepping on her hands twice.

"You always ruin everything!" cried Diane, glaring at Gwen.

"I found two missing kids!" Gwen shook the paper. "See?"

Suddenly Diane grabbed the paper and ran away with it. Gwen cried out, and Sendi raced after Diane.

Sweat soaked Sendi's clothes, and her mouth turned bone-dry. "Give that back right now, Diane!" shouted Sendi.

Diane ducked behind a low bush and held the paper high. "Stop chasing me or I'll rip it up. I mean it!"

Sendi stopped short and Gwen crashed into her.

"Give back my paper," said Gwen.

"No way!" cried Diane. "If you really did find two missing kids, I'm going to help get them back to their families."

"I did."

"Who?" asked Sendi, her heart sinking a little.

"I am going with you," said Diane firmly. "Why should you get to have all the fun?"

"It's Tommy and Star," whispered Gwen to Sendi. "I just know I'm right this time."

Sendi doubled her fists. "I'll get the paper from Diane."

"No. She'll tear it up if you try, and that's my only copy. I don't have the information written in my book." Gwen patted the book in her shorts pocket. "We'll have to let Diane help."

Sendi wrinkled her nose. She wanted to rush at Diane, knock her to the ground, and grab the paper, but she stood quietly beside Gwen and watched the look of triumph wash over Diane's face.

"Well?" asked Diane.

"Bring the paper and you can go with us," said Gwen with a great sigh.

Diane held the paper close, and her blue eyes flashed with excitement. A twig was caught in her long dark hair. "I will carry the paper. Where are we going?"

"Over on the next block to the Langstons." Gwen rolled her eyes, and Sendi nodded her understanding.

With a shout Diane ran on ahead. Sendi plucked at Gwen's arm.

"What did your parents say about . . . about your . . . you know what?"

Gwen's face turned a cherry red. "It's a long story."

Sendi stopped and jabbed her fists on her hips. "I know something's up. Tell me right now."

"Well . . ." Gwen twisted the toe of her tennis shoe against a weed growing up from the crack in the sidewalk. Ants crawled over an apple core.

"Well?"

Gwen looked Sendi in the eye. "They are my real parents. They took me to the hospital and showed me the records and everything. I was wrong."

Sendi's heart sank. Was Gwen wrong about the Langstons too? "What about the adoption paper thing?"

"They were going to adopt a baby, but they got pregnant with me and so they didn't adopt." Gwen shrugged, and then flipped back her hair. "They said they didn't think they'd ever give birth to a baby. So they prayed about it and put their names in for adoption. When they had me, they said they'd let someone else have the baby that might've been theirs since there weren't enough babies to go around to everyone that wanted them. They said God blessed them with me."

Sendi turned away. "You were wrong about everything, weren't you?"

"Yes." Gwen held out a hand and her eyes were round and serious. "But not the Langstons! I promise!"

Diane's feet slapped against the sidewalk as she ran back to Sendi and Gwen. "What's going on? What happened?"

"Nothing!" said Gwen before Sendi could speak. "Let's go. Coming, Sendi?"

She tugged her tee shirt over her shorts and finally nodded. "But if you're wrong, I'm getting away from there fast."

"I'm not wrong. Trust me. I know."

"Let's go!" Diane pranced around, the paper held tightly in one hand. "I got to get back to play in my tree house while it's still my turn."

Her face set, Gwen lifted her head, and then ran down the sidewalk with her hands swinging at her sides.

"Hey, wait for me!" cried Diane, racing after her.

Sendi hesitated a second and sprinted after the others. Hot wind blew against her and she wanted to stop in the shade, but she kept running until she stood with Gwen and

Diane outside the Langstons' door. Traffic sounds from the main highway a block away filled the air.

"I already called the phone number on the paper, and the woman said she'd be here as soon as possible." Gwen looked very proud of herself. "She's flying in from Atlanta."

"How'd you get her to believe you?" asked Diane.

"I sounded very sure of myself and gave her details about the kids," said Gwen.

"Oh my," said Sendi. "What if you're wrong?"

Gwen looked smug. "I'm not wrong."

"Are you ever right?" asked Diane with a short laugh. She pressed the doorbell, and then pressed it again.

"I think I'm going home," whispered Sendi, her eyes glued to the door and her legs trembling.

Suddenly the door opened, and Mrs. Langston stood there dressed in jeans and a tee shirt with Minnie Mouse on it. The smell of freshly baked cookies drifted out from inside. "Yes? What is it now?"

Diane thrust the paper into Gwen's hands and jumped back. "She has something to say!"

"What is it this time?" Mrs. Langston looked at Gwen.

Gwen took a deep breath.

Sendi locked her hands together. Why had she listened to Gwen?

Gwen said all in one breath, "I know you have kids that belong to someone else." She tapped the paper. "I have all the information here. I already called the mother the kids really belong to. She'll be here tomorrow."

Mrs. Langston sagged against the door frame. "Oh my."

Sendi stared at her. Was Mrs. Langston guilty?

Mrs. Langston pushed her hair back from her pale face. "Little girl, do you realize what you've done? You don't even know what you're talking about."

"But I do! It's all right here!"

"Let me see that paper."

Gwen clutched it to her. "You can see it only if I can keep ahold of it. It's my only copy."

Mrs. Langston nodded.

"I'll call the police," said Diane.

"No!" cried Mrs. Langston.

"Not yet," said Gwen, and Sendi knew Gwen was thinking of the last time. She held the paper out. Mrs. Langston read it over and looked at the photo of the two children.

"They do look a little like mine, but those kids aren't Tommy and Star. I gave birth to Tommy and Star and I can prove it. Heaven knows why I should bother, but we must stop that poor woman from making a trip from Atlanta to find out the kids aren't hers."

"Oh, no," whispered Sendi.

"You told me you can't prove they are your children," said Gwen in a weak voice.

"I did not!"

"You said you didn't have their birth certificates," whispered Gwen.

"That's right," said Sendi, stepping closer to Gwen.

"I don't have them here. They're locked in the bank in a safety deposit box."

Diane flung up her arms and laughed loud and long. "I should've known you made another mistake, Gwen McNeeley! Wait'll I tell everybody!" Diane turned and ran, laughing at the top of her lungs.

Sendi felt like creeping away to hide.

"Step inside and let's get this settled," said Mrs. Langston with a ring of authority in her voice. "What is your phone number? I want your parents in on this."

"I'm going home," whispered Sendi.

Gwen turned to her, her eyes wide. "Please stay with me. Please, please, please."

Sendi sighed and nodded and slowly followed Gwen inside the Langston house.

8

Grounded

*H*er heart in her mouth, Sendi tapped on Gwen's bedroom window. A cool morning breeze blew the leaves in the nearby tree. It had rained the night before, cooling down the uncomfortable temperature.

Gwen opened her window and whispered, "I hoped you'd come."

"I rang the doorbell, but Mrs. Lewis wouldn't let me in."

"I know." Gwen sighed loud and long. "I'm grounded and I can't play with anyone or go anywhere for an entire week."

"That's too bad."

"I know." Gwen rubbed her finger over the screen. "I guess I deserve it. I was wrong to jump right in before I really checked my facts. But I was so sure!"

"Yeah."

"I mean, I thought I was absolutely right. I did! Didn't you?"

Sendi shrugged. What could she say? "What did Mrs. Langston do about the woman from Atlanta?"

"Called her and talked to her and told her not to come. Mom and Dad were so upset!" Gwen twisted a strand of dark hair around her finger. "They might not get over this. If I hadn't been wrong about them being my real parents, they might not have taken this so hard."

Sendi moved enough to keep the shrub under the window from scratching her legs. "What're they going to do to you? Beat you?"

"No. Worse."

Sendi trembled. "Lock you in a closet and not feed you or anything?"

Gwen shook her head. "Worse."

"What can be worse?" Sendi rubbed a hand across the cold knot in her stomach. Were they going to kill Gwen?

Gwen leaned her forehead against the screen. "I think they're going to take away all of my material on the missing children." Her voice broke. "I think they're going to make sure I never again as long as I live try to find a missing child and get him back home. That's what I think they're going to do."

"Oh, dear. That's too bad." But maybe it was for the best. Maybe children of the neighborhood would be safe now.

Suddenly Gwen jumped up. "I have it!"

Sendi backed away from the window and looked around quickly to make sure no one was watching or listening. "What're you talking about?"

"I know what I'm going to do!" Gwen unhooked the half-screen, carefully turned it, and pulled it inside. Suddenly Sendi could see her without all the tiny squares all over her.

Sendi twisted a strand of tangled blonde hair around her fingers. "Are you going to run away?"

"Oh, no! Never!"

"Do you want me to crawl in and talk to you?"

"No. I'm not allowed to have company." Gwen ran to her dresser and carried back an armload of papers. "Here. Take these."

Sendi took them, looked at them, and then gasped, "This is your pile of missing children."

"Yes. And you're going to take everything over to your house so Mom and Dad can't destroy all my stuff. You will take over my job while I'm grounded."

"No! I can't!"

"Sure you can. Just study the pictures and read the descriptions and be on the lookout for anyone fitting the descriptions. It's easy."

"I will not find missing kids and be embarrassed by finding the wrong ones."

"Then just take everything to your house and keep it for me. The work will have to wait until I am once again a free person."

"I don't know." Sendi looked at the bundle of papers.

"And remember to pray for them. I will, for sure."

Sendi nodded. She had remembered to last night, especially for the Atlanta woman's children.

"Listen, Sendi." Gwen lowered her voice. "I might be onto something already."

Sendi's heart sank.

"Pete. I'm sure that top picture is Pete. You'll have to check it out for me."

"No!" cried Sendi.

"But poor Pete! What if he was stolen? His poor mother," whispered Gwen.

Sendi thought of her little friend with the big sad eyes, but then she remembered the humiliation last night when she'd been asked to leave once Gwen's parents had arrived. "I don't know, Gwen."

"Just think about it and pray about it."

Several minutes later Sendi piled the last of Gwen's stuff in a box that fit under her bed. She sat on the edge of her bed and stared at the box. Should she look at the picture to see if it was Pete?

She shook her head. He was with his dad and they seemed happy together. At least Pete had a dad and that was more than she had.

Maybe she should start a box of missing dads.

"But I wouldn't know him if I saw him," she muttered.

"Know who?"

She jumped up and scowled at Diane standing in the doorway. "What're you doing in here? You can't just walk into a person's house!"

"The back door was unlocked. Anybody could walk in." Diane looked around, and then sank down on the edge of the bed near Sendi's pillow. "Who wouldn't you know if you saw him?"

Shivers ran up and down Sendi's spine. "None of your business!"

"Do you have a boyfriend?"

"No!"

"A dad?" asked Diane.

"Get out of my bedroom and out of my house!" shouted Sendi.

"I just wanted to know if you want to play with me since Gwen is grounded."

"No," said Sendi.

"Aren't you bored?"

"Maybe."

"I am." Diane touched the box with the tip of her sandal.

Sendi held her breath. Why hadn't she pushed it under the bed?

Diane jumped up and picked up the stack of coloring books off Sendi's dresser. "Hey, let's color. I'm really good at it."

Sendi tried to grab the books from Diane, but Diane turned away and gripped them to her chest. What would she do if Diane found her birth certificate? Sweat popped out across her face and on the palms of her hands even though a cool breeze blew through the window. "Put those books back right now!"

Diane just laughed and leafed through the pile.

Frantically Sendi lunged at Diane and snatched at the pile.

"Hey, stop that!" Diane stumbled and the books fell to the floor, spreading out to cover most of the tiny floor space. The animal coloring book rested on Diane's left foot.

"I'll get them!" cried Sendi as she dropped to the floor and tried to pick all of them up at once. Her hand closed over the animal one at the same time that Diane's did. Sendi's heart crashed to her feet. "Give that back," she whispered hoarsely.

"What is wrong with you, Sendi? You act like I found a terrible secret." Diane flipped open the book, and it fell open right at the birth certificate.

With a strangled cry Sendi reached for it, but Diane sprang away with it. "Be careful with it! Don't tear it!" Sendi wanted to grab it from Diane, but she knew Diane would hang on tighter and make it rip.

"Why don't you want me to read your birth certificate?" asked Diane.

"It's mine and it's private." It was hard to talk through the tightness of her throat. "Please, just give it to me. Please."

"I will in a minute." Diane's blue eyes twinkled with mischief. "In a minute, as soon as I read it."

Sendi dropped to the floor on her knees with a groan that tore from deep inside her.

Diane looked closer at the paper. "Sendi Lee Mason. Mother: Janice Jean Mason."

Sendi's ears rang.

"Your mother? But you said she was dead!"

Sendi clasped her hands over her thudding heart.

Diane looked back at the certificate. "Mother's age: Thirteen years. Are you serious? Thirteen?"

The room spun and Sendi reached weakly for the paper, but Diane stepped away.

"Father: Unknown." Diane's voice faded away and she looked at Sendi. "Oh my."

Tears slipped down Sendi's ashen face.

"I never knew anybody that didn't know who their own father was."

Sendi held out a shaky hand, and Diane slowly gave her the certificate. Sendi pressed it to her chest and rocked back and forth.

Diane sank to the bed and locked her arms over her heart. "Stop crying, Sendi. Please, stop crying."

But the tears continued to fall.

"Janice Jean Mason is your mother."

Sendi's eyes flew open and the tears stopped. "No!"

"Yes!"

"No! Don't say that!" shouted Sendi.

"But it's true. She's not your sister. She's your mother!"

"It's a secret! A secret that I promised not to tell!"

Diane shivered. "That's a terrible secret. Why doesn't she want anyone to know she's your mom?"

"She wants a new start. She doesn't want to explain about me. She wants people to think she's wonderful because she's taking care of her 'little sister.' She wants a new home and new friends and a husband if she can find a man who'll care for her."

"My mom wants everybody to know she's my mom and my two sisters' mom and my two brothers' mom. She would never keep that a secret. My dad wouldn't either."

Sendi took a deep, shuddering breath. "I promised I'd keep her secret." Sendi looked pleadingly at Diane. "Will you keep my mom's secret?"

Diane narrowed her eyes. "Maybe."

"Please!"

"I might."

"We'll have to move if you don't," whispered Sendi.

Diane fingered the hem of her tee shirt. "I might keep it a secret. If . . ."

"If what?"

"If you'll be my friend," said Diane.

Sendi frowned. "What d' you mean?"

"Be my friend."

"Yes! Anything! I will!" cried Sendi.

"I mean *my* friend."

"I said I would."

"Not Gwen's. Not anybody else's. Just mine." Diane tapped her chest.

"Oh."

Diane picked up the pillow and hugged it to her. "I have no friends. I get lonely and bored. If we can be friends and play together and go places together and all that stuff that friends do, I'll keep your secret."

Sendi slowly slipped her birth certificate back in the animal coloring book, picked up the other books, and set them on her dresser. Could she do what Diane asked? Sendi's heart sank. She knew she'd have to. Mom . . . Janice had said she was desperate for a new start in life. For Janice she'd have to do it.

"Well?"

Sendi slowly nodded. "I'll be your friend."

Diane leaped up and down. "Yeh!" Suddenly she stopped. "Now I'll tell you a secret that you can't tell anyone."

"You don't have to," said Sendi.

"I want to. Then we'll be even." Diane stepped close to Sendi and lowered her voice. "Sometimes I suck my thumb."

"Oh." It didn't seem like much of a secret.

"I'm nine years old and going into fourth grade! Nobody that old still sucks their thumb!"

"It's a dumb secret."

"But you can't tell anyone. I mean it. If you do, I'll tell yours."

Sendi sighed and sank to the edge of the bed. "I won't tell anyone. I promise."

"Listen!" Diane lifted her hand, and then ran to the window. "Oh, my mom's calling me. I have to go, but I'll be back. We'll play together all the rest of the day. You can come to my house and play with my stuff. But only if I say so." She ran from the room and Sendi heard the back door slam.

"Will she keep the secret?" she whispered.

For a long time she sat with her head in her hands. How could she survive now that Diane knew the truth?

What had Gwen said about surviving? Sendi frowned thoughtfully.

"God sent Jesus to help us," Gwen had said when Sendi had asked how she could survive her punishment. "Jesus loves me and you and all people. He's like family, always there to help and love you."

Sendi remembered one of Momma's friends had talked about Jesus all the time and said that He could do anything.

Sendi lifted her head and whispered, "Jesus, I need You. Gwen said she'd teach me about You, but she can't right now and I can't wait. I don't know what to do about every- thing. Please, help me."

She couldn't explain it even to herself, but she knew He was there with her to help her and comfort her. She no longer felt alone. From deep inside she felt as if she'd just been hugged close by Love.

9

Pete

S endi reached for the box of Gwen's material on missing children to shove it under the bed, and then stopped. The top picture did look like Pete. Was it possible? Her breath caught in her throat.

"No! I'm not going to be another Gwen McNeeley!"

With a hard push she shoved the box out of sight under her bed. "There." She stayed on her knees beside her bed and looked at the sheet hanging down enough to hide the box from sight. Gwen was only imagining things again, and it couldn't really be Pete on the poster.

But what if it was?

"It's not!"

But what if it was?

"It can't be!"

But what if it was?

Sendi grabbed the box and slid it back out. The sheet flipped over the box and dropped back in place. "It won't be Pete. I know it won't be."

She picked up the paper and read the description and looked at the face. "That's not Pete." Relieved she started to drop the poster back in place, and then stopped when she spotted the next one in line. Slowly she picked it up and let the other one flutter to the floor.

Sad eyes looked up at her from a tiny, thin face. She read, "Isaac Thomas Bender, four, was abducted by his father from the home of his custodial mother on April 7. Isaac has blond hair and blue eyes. He has a birthmark on the inside of his left wrist—a small, red circle about half the size of a dime. He may be in Missouri."

But he wasn't in Missouri. He was just

down the block. Sendi's stomach tightened and a bitter taste filled her mouth. "Pete," she whispered hoarsely. She glanced at the year on the poster to see it was last year. Last year Pete would've been four and this year he's five. A picture of him holding up his little hand with his fingers spread flashed in her mind.

"Oh, Pete."

Sendi leaned weakly against her bed. What could she do? Mom had said not to get involved. Gwen was grounded and she couldn't help. Dare she call the number on the paper?

She groaned. No way would she make the same mistakes Gwen had made. Maybe she should tear up the picture and forget the whole thing. No one would ever know. Gwen would never know. She thought the other picture was Pete. Gwen didn't know about the birthmark on Pete . . . Isaac's wrist.

"What'll I do?" The words hung heavy in the air around her. "I won't do anything."

If she were stolen, she'd want someone to help get her back home.

"I have to help him," she whispered weakly. "Jesus, help me to know what to do to help Pete."

Slowly she stood up. Her knees buckled,

and she almost fell, but caught herself on the side of the bed. Another paper caught her attention and she picked it up. Thoughtfully she looked at the bold words, CHILD FIND, INC., A NATIONAL CHILD-LOCATING AGENCY. A toll-free phone number was printed beside it. Maybe she could call the number and tell them about Pete, and they would know what to do.

But she had no telephone.

"I won't do anything."

Pete's wide eyes stared up at her from the photo, and she knew she had to do something.

"Gwen! I'll call from Gwen's house!" Sendi folded the paper about Pete with the paper on Child Find and stuffed them both in the pocket of her shorts. Trembling she shoved the box back under the bed and ran from her room into the living room, the kitchen, and out the back door. A warm wind swirled a piece of paper across the backyard to stick against the weeds beside the sandbox.

"And just where do you think you're going?"

Sendi whirled around to find Diane standing a few feet away with her hands on her hips, her eyes flashing. Sendi swallowed hard. "I wanted to talk to Gwen."

"You can't. I won't let you."

"You can't stop me!"

Smugly Diane looked around. "There are the Hansens. I'll go tell them just who Janice Mason is."

"No! Wait!" Sendi stepped back against her house. "I won't talk to Gwen right now. I'll go back inside and watch TV or something."

"You do that and when I get back from shopping with Mom, I'll come get you and we'll play together."

With her head down Sendi walked back inside and leaned against the door. Anger at Diane rushed through her, and she doubled her fists. How could she even pretend to be friends with that girl?

Her bottom lip quivered. For Janice she had to do what Diane said. But no way would she stay inside just because Diane said she had to. She ran to the front window and watched Diane climb in the station wagon with her family. "I'll just make sure I'm back before she is."

She slipped out her front door and raced down the sidewalk toward Pete's house. Maybe he *wanted* to be with his dad. If she was with her dad, she wouldn't want anyone to take her away. Would she?

At Pete's house she hesitated, and then

knocked timidly on the front door. Jack Thomason opened the door and frowned down at her.

It took her a while to find her voice. "Could Pete come out to play with me?"

Just then Pete stuck his head around his dad's jean-clad leg. "Hi, Sendi."

"Hi, Pete. Want to play?"

"Sure."

"He can't," said his dad. "Sorry."

"Please, Dad!"

Sendi touched her pocket that held the information on Pete, who really was Isaac Thomas Bender. "We'll stay right in the yard," said Sendi.

"No."

Pete stuck out his bottom lip and sniffed as if he were going to cry.

"No!" said his dad in a firm voice. He looked back at Sendi. "I don't want you to come back again."

Pete burst into tears just as his dad slammed the door. Slowly Sendi walked away, her hand over her pocket. Gwen had told her that stolen children often didn't lead normal lives and couldn't have close friends.

"I have to help him," she said in a voice as firm as Jack Thomason's.

A few minutes later, Sendi stood outside Gwen's window and called softly, "Gwen. Where are you?"

Gwen's head appeared and she smiled. "Did you find Pete?"

Wind blew hair across Sendi's face and she pushed it back. "I found him."

Gwen gasped. "You did?"

"I have to come in."

"But you can't."

"I have to. Take out the screen, and I'll crawl through the window."

Gwen thought for a minute and then carefully removed the screen.

Sendi looked around, her heart in her mouth. No one was in sight. But how did she know eyes weren't watching from windows all over the neighborhood?

"Hurry, Sendi!" Gwen reached out to grip Sendi's hand.

Sendi jumped up, flopped over the window ledge, and then wriggled across and dropped to the carpeted floor.

"Tell me everything! Quick!" cried Gwen.

Sendi dug the papers from her pocket, unfolded them, and handed them to Gwen.

"But this isn't the right boy!"

"Yes, it is. The other one wasn't." Quickly Sendi told Gwen about the birthmark and how she'd come to see it.

"I'm so excited! I'm going to call his mom right now!"

Sendi grabbed her arm. "No!"

"No?"

"I've thought and thought about it. I know we should try to help missing kids get back to their families, but we can't make mistakes like you've done so far."

Gwen flushed and nodded. "So, what will we do?"

"Call Child Find. They'll know how to tell the mother without making trouble, and they'll know how to get Pete . . . Isaac away from his dad without hurting Pete." Sendi tapped on the paper. "Here's a number. That's why I had to come in."

"Oh, Sendi, you're wonderful!"

Sendi grinned and ducked her head. No one had ever said that to her before. Finally she looked up again. "Go call right now."

Gwen took a step toward the door, and then stopped. "No. You call, Sendi. This is your find. You call." With a flourish she held the paper out to Sendi. Finally Sendi took it, her heart hammering hard against her rib cage.

"Mrs. Lewis is watching TV so we'll call from Mom and Dad's room." Gwen crept across the hall into the larger bedroom.

Sendi followed and took the light blue receiver that Gwen held out to her. Sweat on her palms made the phone slippery. She punched the numbers and waited, only to hear a busy signal. She dropped the receiver back in place with a clatter. "It's busy."

"Then try again in a minute."

But now the butterflies in her stomach fluttered so hard she didn't know if she could.

"So, Pete is really Isaac Thomas Bender. Wow!" Gwen read the paper aloud in a voice filled with awe. "Almost a year now I've been hunting for missing kids, and none that I thought were missing really were. But Pete is. My months of struggle have paid off. Maybe now Mom and Dad will let me keep my stuff on missing kids."

"They won't if you don't tell them that you'll let someone take over after you find them. Like Child Find."

Gwen thought about that a long time and finally nodded. "You're right. I can't do like I've been doing. It causes too much trouble." She picked up the receiver again and thrust it into Sendi's hand. "Try again."

Sendi's finger shook, but she was able to punch the numbers. The phone on the other end rang and a woman's voice answered, "Child Find . . . may I help you?"

In a squeaky voice, Sendi told about Pete and gave all the information the woman asked for. Sendi gave her Gwen's phone number, and Gwen nodded that it was all right. Finally Sendi hung up and sank weakly to the chair in the corner of the room.

Gwen dropped to the carpet and rested her chin on the arm of the chair. "What'd they say?"

"She said that we must stay away from Isaac. She called him Isaac instead of Pete. She said to stay away from Isaac so we don't make his dad suspicious. She said they'll send someone right over to check it out. After they're positive, then they'll call Isaac's mother and tell her. She's been waiting a year to find Isaac."

"Oh, Sendi! We found a missing child!" Tears sprang to Gwen's eyes. "This is the happiest day of my life. Wait'll I tell Mom and Dad! And Mrs. Lewis."

"But don't say anything until Pete is safe with his mom."

"It'll be hard, but I won't say a word."

Sendi pushed herself up. "I have to go before Diane gets back."

"Diane? Why?" asked Gwen.

Sendi slipped across the hall, searching frantically for an answer. "I told her I'd play with her when she gets back from shopping."

"Does she know about Pete?"

"No! And I will never tell her! You keep the papers about Pete and Child Find so Diane can't grab them from me," said Sendi.

"I will. Thanks for coming, Sendi. See you when my punishment is over." Gwen helped Sendi out the window and carefully snapped the half-screen in place.

Sendi looked all around, and then raced to her house and slipped inside the back door.

Smells of Janice's morning coffee and toast hung in the air.

"I made it." She smiled and walked to the refrigerator for an ice cream bar.

10

Love

S endi slowly chewed the bite of hamburger as she looked around Great Burgers. She and Janice were the only people in the kiddy section. She counted six others in the adult section and five people behind the counter and in the kitchen. Smells of grilled burgers mixed with french fries drifted across the room and over the brightly decorated partition to the kiddy section. Over the background music, Sendi heard the laughter from the workers.

"I probably shouldn't have used my money

like this," said Janice with a loud sigh as she picked up a french fry. She'd walked in the house just after work, changed into shorts and a loose top, and told Sendi they were going out for supper. "I was too tired to cook today. This has been a long week."

Sendi agreed. Being friends with Diane was hard work.

"You've been pretty quiet for the last few days, Sendi. Are you still moping about moving away from Momma's?" asked Janice.

"No." But maybe she was. If they still lived with her grandma, she'd never have had this trouble with Diane. But she wouldn't have learned that Jesus loved her. Nor would she have been able to help Pete.

"I called Momma this morning," said Janice.

Sendi's mouth dropped open. "You did?"

"I wasn't going to, but I missed her too much. I've never lived away from her before, you know."

"Does she miss us?" whispered Sendi.

"Yes. But she has her friends and her work, so she'll be all right without us." Janice played with the straw in her Coke. "And we'll be all right without her. We have to be."

Sendi fingered her napkin.

Janice took a sip of her Coke. "Maybe I was wrong about . . . about . . . you know."

Sendi sat very still. "What?"

"About me . . . you." Janice shrugged. "Well, I guess I do deserve a fresh start, even if I had to lie to get it. We're doing all right."

Sendi took another bite of hamburger and chewed slowly. So far she wasn't doing all right with Diane and the terrible secret between them.

"Did you see Gwen today?" asked Janice.

"No. She's still grounded," said Sendi.

"I heard about her trying to turn in two kids that she thought were kidnapped. A woman that came in for a sun streaking gave all the details. Sun streaking. She could've sat out in this sun and had it done for free." Janice took a long sip of her Coke. "But back to Gwen. I can't believe she'd do such a dumb thing."

Sendi just kept chewing. She'd talked to Gwen through her window yesterday for just a short time.

"Have you seen Pete . . . I mean Isaac?" Gwen had asked.

"No. You know we're supposed to stay

away from there. The woman from Child Find said these things take time."

"I hope it doesn't take too much longer." Gwen sighed. "Have you studied more of the missing children papers?"

"No. Well, a little." Mostly she'd been kept busy by Diane.

"I'll get my stuff back once Mom and Dad forget about my mistake and hear about finding Pete," said Gwen.

"Do you think they'll let you keep looking for missing kids?" asked Sendi.

"Sure. They'll get busy with their lives and leave me with Mrs. Lewis. Then I'll get back to work. I can't wait to hear about Pete."

Sendi had walked away, promising to stop by again. She had wanted to walk past Pete's house just to see if she could see him, but Diane had called her.

Janice tapped the back of Sendi's hand. "Hey, are you daydreaming?"

Sendi jumped and grinned sheepishly. "Just thinking about Gwen."

"Gwen!" Janice rolled her eyes. "Your new friend, Diane, seems more your type."

Sendi bit back a groan.

"She gets a little sassy at times," said Janice.

Just then the door opened, and Sendi glanced up to find Diane walking in with her family. Sendi wanted to slide under the table and hide, but Diane spotted her and ran to her, grinning and showing all of her sharp, white teeth.

"Hi, Sendi. Hi, Janice."

"Hello, Diane." Janice smiled. She'd told Diane to call her Janice, but Sendi knew that if Janice learned that Diane had discovered her secret, she'd never speak to her or be nice to her.

Sendi forced out a soft hello before she pretended a great interest in her leftover french fries.

"I'll be over early tomorrow," said Diane. "I want you to go to church with us. My folks said you could. Is that all right with you, Janice?"

Janice shrugged her plump shoulders. "It's really up to Sendi."

Sendi had promised to go to church with Gwen.

"Well?" said Diane, leaning close to Sendi.

SENDI LEE MASON

Sendi glanced at Janice, and then back down at her french fry. It was cold and looked greasy. She pushed it into her mouth and tasted the salt first and then the grease. She never did taste the potato.

Diane leaned closer. "Well?"

"What's wrong with you, Sendi?" snapped Janice. "Answer the girl."

Sendi took a deep breath. "I don't want to go."

Diane narrowed her eyes. "But I want you to."

Sendi froze.

Janice stood up and picked up her purse. "I've been thinking about going to church myself."

Sendi's brows shot up. Momma sometimes had gone to church, and she had a few times, but Janice never had.

"We might both go." Janice patted Diane's shoulder. "We'll see."

Sendi dashed for the door before Diane could say another word. Heat struck her full force after the air-conditioned restaurant and she gasped. She wished back the cool weather of a few days ago.

Janice unlocked the car, slipped under

118

the steering wheel, and then reached to unlock Sendi's door.

The handle burned her fingers as she opened the door. The car smelled like gasoline. It was too hot to lean against the vinyl seat. Sendi made a face. "It's so hot. Can we go swimming today, Mom?"

Janice gasped and darted a look around. "Sendi! You promised!"

Sendi slapped her hand over her mouth and stared fearfully at Janice. "I didn't mean to call you Mom. It just slipped out."

Janice sighed heavily. "It's all right. I miss hearing it."

"Diane knows."

"What?" The word ended on a note that could break a glass.

Sendi trembled. She'd not meant to tell, but it'd just popped out.

Janice patted her face with a wadded-up tissue. "How'd she find out? Did you tell her after I asked, begged you not to?"

"No. She's just sort of . . . learned."

"Does anyone else know?"

"No."

"Not even Gwen?"

"No."

Janice gripped the steering wheel tight enough to turn her knuckles white. "How did Diane find out?"

Sendi sank low in her seat.

"How, Sendi Lee Mason?"

Sendi shivered and covered her face.

"Tell me right now, Sendi. Right now!"

Slowly Sendi sat up and, with clouded eyes, faced Janice. "She saw my birth certificate."

Janice shook her head. "Your birth certificate is lost. I had it when you enrolled in kindergarten, and then lost it."

"I have it."

Janice took a deep breath, looked out into space, and then looked over at Sendi again. "Why didn't you give it to me?"

Sendi picked at her thumbnail. "I wanted it."

"You wanted it?"

"Yes."

"Why?"

Sendi swallowed hard. "To look at."

"But why?"

"So I'd know I wasn't an alien nor hatched from an egg."

"Who said anything like that?"

"Kids."

Janice was quiet for a long time. "Did you get teased about me?"

"No."

"About what?"

Sendi watched a car pull away from beside them. Finally she twisted around and faced Janice. "About never having a dad and about being weird and living with a momma and a mom."

"Oh. I didn't know. I had no idea." Nervously Janice pushed her hair back. "I guess I was so busy protecting myself and my feelings that I never learned how to be a mother and protect you."

Sendi saw tears fill Janice's eyes. It made her feel strange to think Mom was crying because of her. "That's all right."

"No. No, it's not all right."

Just then Diane and her family walked out the door. Diane ran to Sendi. "We'll play when we get home."

Sendi nodded weakly.

Diane ran to the station wagon and climbed in with her brothers and sisters. She waved as they drove away. Sendi didn't wave back.

Janice narrowed her eyes. "Now, why hasn't Diane told anyone about me?"

Sendi rubbed an unsteady hand across her mouth.

"Sendi?"

She shrugged.

"You know, don't you?"

"Yes."

"Then tell me. Now."

Reluctantly she told Janice.

Janice's face hardened. "We'll see about that."

Sendi locked her fingers in her lap. "I shouldn't have told you!"

"It's a good thing you did."

"But she'll tell everyone."

"We'll see about that too," Janice said grimly as she started the car and drove toward home. "I have thought entirely too much about myself and not enough about you." At a stoplight Janice touched Sendi's hand, and Sendi's heart leaped. "You're my little girl, and it's time I started being a mother to you. I'm not your sister. I'm your mother."

Sendi sat very still and waited. Maybe Mom would say she loved her the way moms on TV did.

The light changed, and Janice drove the few blocks home in silence.

Disappointed, Sendi slipped out of the car to find Gwen waiting for her. "Hi. I thought you were grounded," said Sendi.

"My dad said I could get off early for good behavior and because of Pete." Gwen laughed, and then turned to Janice. "Hi."

"Hello, Gwen." Janice walked to the front door and slipped inside.

Gwen grabbed Sendi's hands and danced her around the yard. "Wait'll you hear!"

"What?" Sendi's stomach was still in knots over Diane, but Gwen's excitement made her curious.

"Child Find called me a while ago. They wanted to speak to you. I explained about us working together and that you weren't there, so she told me."

Sendi squeezed Gwen's hands tight. "And?"

"And Pete . . . Isaac is back with his mother! His dad is going to try to work out an arrangement to be near him, but he promised never to take him again. He said he'd been desperate because he wanted Isaac with him so much. Mrs. Bender said she wouldn't press charges against him."

"I'm glad. Now Isaac has both parents around."

Just then the door opened and Janice walked out. She stopped beside Sendi and rested her hand on Sendi's shoulder. "Hello, Gwen. I want you to know something."

Sendi stiffened.

"Sendi is my daughter," said Janice.

Gwen gasped and Sendi stopped breathing.

"I'm her mother, not her sister."

Gwen's mouth dropped open. So did Sendi's.

"I've told you our secret, and one of these days I'll have the courage to tell everyone."

"I'll keep it a secret as long as you want," said Gwen.

Sendi touched Janice's hand.

"Sendi's dad lives in the West somewhere."

Sendi froze. Mom was actually talking about Dad!

"And he wants to pretend he doesn't have a daughter, just like I was trying to do." Janice looked into Sendi's eyes. "I'm sorry. I hate to think about your dad. Maybe someday I can tell you more about him."

Sendi nodded, unable to speak. She had

a real dad and Mom knew who he was and where he was. Suddenly she remembered the day in her room when she had asked Jesus to help work everything out. He had! "Thank You, Jesus. I love You," she said under her breath.

Once again Janice looked at Gwen. "I do have a daughter, and I am going to try to act like a mother from now on." She turned teary eyes to Sendi. "And that's a promise."

Sendi hugged Janice tight. "I love you, Mom."

Janice bent down and kissed the top of Sendi's head. "I love you."

Sendi's heart soared and she hugged Mom tighter.

"I think I'll go home," said Gwen in a tiny voice.

"Wait!" Janice pushed Sendi toward Gwen. "Sendi wants to go with you. She's been wanting to play with you for a long time."

Sendi glanced toward Diane's house just as Diane walked out the door. "I can't play with her."

"Why not?" asked Janice.

"Because of Diane."

Janice chuckled drily. "Go play with Gwen."

"Are you sure, Mom?"

Janice nodded, and then shot a look at Diane. "I'll take care of one little problem first."

Sendi laughed and caught Mom's hand. "I'll go with you. Come on, Gwen."